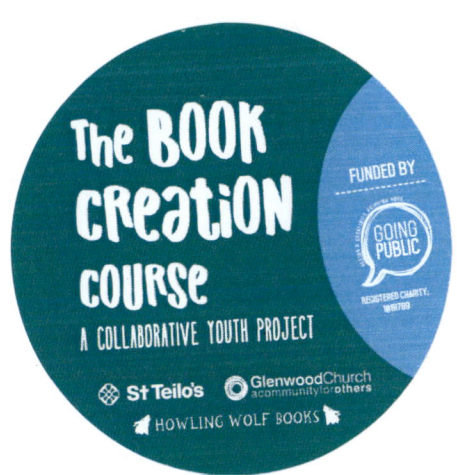

The other group loved rabbits. They were called The Storm Raider Rabbits.

Next, they had a beauty competition.

The dogs all wore tuxedos but the rabbits won with ten votes to two.

Lastly they started to have a fight.

The rabbits did flying kicks.

The rabbits realised that the dogs loved nature too. Maybe we're not so different after all? Do you want to go for a swim?" They all said at the same time!

Printed in Great Britain
by Amazon